World of Reptiles

Boa Constrictors

by Matt Doeden

Consultants:
The Staff of Reptile Gardens
Rapid City, South Dakota

Mankato, Minnesota

Bridgestone Books are published by Capstone Press,
151 Good Counsel Drive, P.O. Box 669, Mankato, Minnesota 56002.
www.capstonepress.com

Library of Congress Cataloging-in-Publication Data
Doeden, Matt.
  Boa constrictors / by Matt Doeden.
    p. cm.—(Bridgestone Books. World of Reptiles.)
    Includes bibliographical references (p. 23) and index.
    ISBN 0-7368-3729-9 (hardcover)
  1. Boa constrictor—Juvenile literature. I. Title. II. Series.
  QL666.O63D637 2005
  597.96'7—dc22   2004014478

Summary: A brief introduction to boa constrictors including what they look like, where they live, what they eat, how they produce young, and dangers boas face.

Editorial Credits
Heather Adamson, editor; Enoch Peterson, book designer; Ted Williams, cover designer;
    Erin Scott, illustrator; Jo Miller, photo researcher; Scott Thoms, photo editor

Photo Credits
Bruce Coleman Inc/Hans Reinhard, 1, 6
Corbis/Joe McDonald, 12; Michael & Patricia Fogden, 10
James E. Gerholdt, 20
McDonald Wildlife Photography/Joe McDonald, cover
Minden Pictures/ZSSD, 16
Peter Arnold/Martin Wendler, 18
Ron Kimball Stock/Javier Flores, 4

Table of Contents

Boa Constrictors

A boa constrictor wraps its long body around its **prey**. The snake squeezes, or **constricts**, the prey to death. Then, the boa constrictor uncurls to eat its meal.

Boa constrictors are **cold-blooded** reptiles. Their body temperatures are the same as the temperatures of their surroundings. Reptiles also have scales and grow from eggs.

Boa constrictors are related to anacondas and pythons. They all kill prey by squeezing.

◄ Boa constrictors have strong bodies. They can wrap their bodies tightly around branches or prey.

What Boa Constrictors Look Like

Boa constrictors are long, thick snakes. They have muscular bodies. The middle of a boa's body is often wider than its head. Most common boas grow to be 6 to 8 feet (1.8 to 2.4 meters) long.

Boas are covered with scales. They have a pattern of markings along their bodies. The common boa constrictor is tan with brown saddle-shaped markings. Other kinds of boas may be green, brown, red, or black. Each kind of boa has different markings.

◄ A boa constrictor's markings help it blend with its surroundings.

Boa Constrictor Range Map

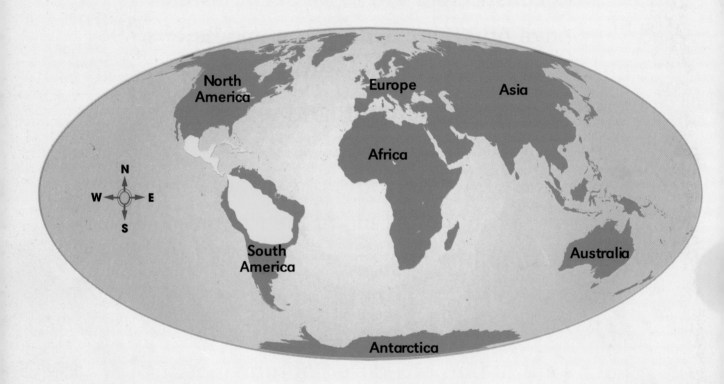

☐ Where Boa Constrictors Live

Boa Constrictors in the World

Boa constrictors live in the rain forests of Central and South America. Most boas live in the northern half of South America. Some kinds of boas live as far north as Mexico.

Some boa constrictors live on islands. St. Lucia boas live on St. Lucia Island in the Caribbean. Tobaga Island boas live only on one island near Panama.

◄ Boa constrictors live in Central and South America.

Boa Constrictor Habitats

Most boas live in rain forest habitats. They climb and swim in the many trees and ponds. Boas also have markings that match the rain forest surroundings.

Some boas live in underground burrows or holes. The boas come out of these burrows to find food. They also leave these holes to warm themselves in the sun.

◄ Boa constrictors climb roots and trees in rain forests. They wait for prey to pass by.

What Boa Constrictors Eat

Boas eat animals that are small enough for them to swallow. Boas eat rats, monkeys, lizards, bats, birds, and wild pigs. Boas even eat young crocodiles.

A boa kills its prey by **suffocating** it. The boa wraps its powerful body around the prey. Every time the prey breathes, the boa constricts its muscles a little more. Soon, the prey cannot breathe and dies. The boa then swallows the prey head first.

◀ A boa wraps its body around a rat. Boas suffocate their prey by squeezing.

Life Cycle of a Boa Constrictor

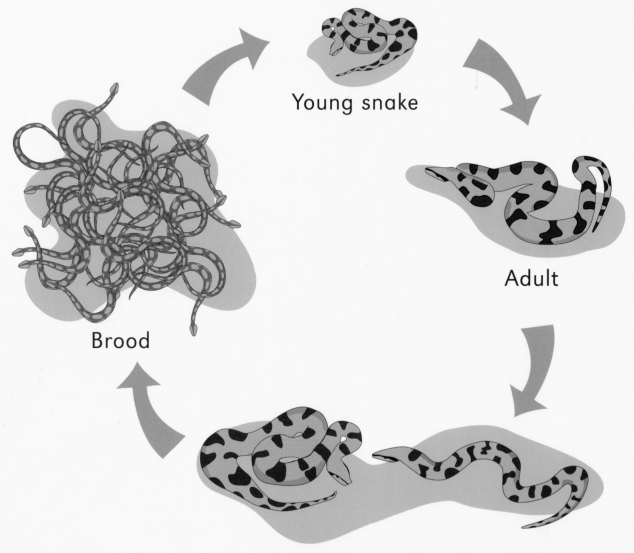

Young snake

Adult

Mating pair

Brood

Producing Young

Boa constrictors **mate** about once a year. Female boas make a scent to attract males. Boas do not stay together after they mate. For a few months, the female boa carries her young in thin egg sacs inside her body.

Newborn boas hatch inside the mother and are born live. As many as 50 snakes may be born at a time. The group of young snakes is called a brood. At birth, most boas are already more than 1 foot (0.3 meter) long.

Growing Up

Young boas do not stay with their mothers. They must hunt and eat on their own. Young boas often climb trees to eat small birds and frogs.

Young snakes grow fast. Snakes must shed their skin, or **molt,** as they grow. The skin becomes loose. Then, the snake crawls out of the old skin. New skin is underneath.

A newborn brood of South American boas doesn't stay together long. Boas are born ready to live on their own.

Dangers to Boa Constrictors

Young boas have many **predators**. Hawks and other large birds hunt young boas. Crocodiles and large cats also hunt young snakes. Boas grow quite large in their first few months. Not many animals will attack large boas.

People are the biggest danger to boas. Farmers kill boas because the snakes eat their chickens. People hunt boas for their skin and their meat. Even with these dangers, many boas live in the world.

◄ Hunters kill boas for their skin and for their meat.

Amazing Facts about Boa Constrictors

- Boas can hiss very loudly. A boa can make a sound that can be heard more than 50 feet (15 meters) away. Boas make this sound when they feel threatened.
- After swallowing large prey, a boa's body may bulge.
- Boas need a long time to **digest** large prey. It can take a few weeks for a boa to digest a large meal.

A bulge forms in a boa's body after swallowing prey.

Glossary

cold-blooded (KOHLD-BLUHD-id)—having a body temperature that is the same as the surroundings; all reptiles are cold-blooded.

constrict (kuhn-STRIKT)—to squeeze; a boa constrictor constricts its body to suffocate prey.

digest (dye-JEST)—to break down food inside the body

mate (MATE)—to join together to produce young

molt (MOHLT)—to shed an outer layer of skin; boas molt several times as they grow.

predator (PRED-uh-tur)—an animal that hunts other animals for food

prey (PRAY)—an animal hunted for food

suffocate (SUHF-uh-kate)—to kill by cutting off air; a boa suffocates its prey by squeezing until the prey can not breathe.

Read More

O'Hare, Ted. *Boa Constrictors.* Amazing Snakes. Vero Beach, Fla.: Rourke, 2004.

Weber, Valerie. *Boa Constrictors.* World's Largest Snakes. Milwaukee: Gareth Stevens, 2003.

Internet Sites

FactHound offers a safe, fun way to find Internet sites related to this book. All of the sites on FactHound have been researched by our staff.

Here's how:
1. Visit *www.facthound.com*
2. Type in this special code **0736837299** for age-appropriate sites. Or enter a search word related to this book for a more general search.
3. Click on the **Fetch It** button.

FactHound will fetch the best sites for you!

Index